UNSTOPPABLE YOU

"TEENS GUIDE FOR SELF-ESTEEM SOARING"

Audrey Erowo Onemu is a Nigerian. She is an emotional health advocate, a certified self-esteem rising tutor and a girl-ife facilitator.

She has BSC in psychology from Obafemi Awolowo University, Ile Ife and have done different certification trainings/courses on mentoring, counselling as well as girl life coaching. She is a member of mentor her to greatness network.

She frequently coaches'women and girls on self-esteem rising both online and offline as well as mentoring of young teen girls.

She is also a serial volunteer with different non-governmental organizations.

She loves to listen to ever green music, visit green open places, write, read and go for hiking.

UNSTOPPABLE YOU

By AUDREY Erowo Onemu

CONTENTS

DEDICATION

To the unstoppable young ladies exploring the journey of self-discovery, this book is dedicated to you. May these pages be your compass, directing you to embrace the power inside, take off with confidence, and become the extraordinary power that is unapologetically you!

PREFACE

"Unstoppable You: teen girls' guide for self-esteem soaring"is an empowering guide designed to inspire and uplift teenage girls. Through practical advice, relatable anecdotes and actionable exercises, this book aim to cultivate self-esteem, resilience and a strong sense of identity. It navigates the challenges of adolescence, offering tools to build confidence and embrace one' unique strengths, ultimately guiding young girls towards a path of self-discovery and unstoppable personal growth.

Questions you can ask yourself to measure your self-esteem

Ask yourself some of these questions below:

• How do I feel about myself?

• What do I like and dislike about myself?

• What are my strengths and weaknesses?

• How do I cope with challenges and difficulties?

• How do I celebrate my achievements and successes

• How do I treat myself and others?

• How do I express myself and my opinions?

• How do I handle feedback and criticism?

• How do I deal with stress and emotions?

• How do I pursue my goals and dreams?

Chapter One

UNLEASH YOUR INNER SUPERPOWER

Chapter One

Unleash Your Inner Superpower

You have a superpower!

It isn't the capacity to fly, or to understand minds, or to shoot lasers from your eyes. It is something considerably more impressive and significant. Something can assist you with accomplishing your objectives, defeat your difficulties, and experience your fantasies. Something can satisfy you. Something can make you relentless. Your superpower is your confidence!

What is self-esteem?

Self-esteem is the manner by which you feel about yourself. It is the assessment and the demeanor you have towards yourself. It is the worth and the regard you give yourself. It is the affection and the acknowledgment you have for yourself.

For what reason is self-esteem significant?

It is significant on the grounds that it influences all that you do. It influences your thought process, how you feel, how you act, and how you connect with others. It influences your decisions, your activities, your outcomes, and your results. It influences your joy, your well-being and your prosperity.

How does self-esteem work?

It works like a cycle. At the point when you have high self-esteem, you feel much better about

yourself. You have confidence in yourself and your capacities. You are sure and hopeful. You are still up in the air.

You are strong and gutsy. You can confront and defeat any obstructions that come your direction. You can accomplish your objectives and realize your true capacity. You can appreciate and value your life.

At the point when you have low self-esteem, you regret yourself. You question yourself and your capacities. You are uncertain and cynical. You are unmotivated and deterred. You are unfortunate and restless. You can't adapt to any difficulties that come your direction. You can't arrive at your objectives and understand your true capacity. You can't appreciate and value your life.

As may be obvious, self-esteem gigantically affects your life. It can either engage you or cutoff you. It can either lift you up or drag you down. It can either make you relentless or make you stuck.

Fortunately, self-esteem isn't something fixed or long-lasting. It isn't something that you are brought into the world with, no matter what. It isn't something that others can plus or minus away from you. It is something that you can create and get to the next level. It is something that you have some control over and can change.

Setting the stage for building unstoppable self-esteem.

By taking on these standards and outlook shifts, youngster can start their extraordinary excursion toward building and keeping up with sound confidence, empowering them to be persistent in chasing after their fantasies and objectives.

- **Self-Acceptance:** It is the process of recognizing and embracing your true self, including your strength, weaknesses and unique qualities without judgement or self-criticism. It is an important aspect of personal growth and mental well-being. Figure out how to embrace and acknowledge yourself for who you are, understanding that you are one of a kind and commendable similarly as you are.

- **Positive Self-Talk:** Shift from self-analysis to self-consolation by rehearsing positive self-talk. Positive self-talk involves affirming, encouraging and using supportive language when communicating with yourself. It can help boost your self-esteem, confidence, and over all well-being. Supplant negative considerations with certifications that support your certainty.

- **Resisting Generalizations;** Challenge cultural generalizations and assumptions that can restrict your self-esteem. Perceive that you don't need to squeeze into predefined roles to be significant.

- **Strength:** Comprehend that mishaps and disappointments are essential for life.

Develop strength from difficulties and use them as an open door for development.

● **Strong Connections:** Encircle yourself with friends and coaches who inspires and engages you. Sound connections can essentially affect your confidence

● **Self-Empathy:** Indulge yourself with a similar thoughtfulness and sympathy you would propose to another person when in a difficult situation. Self-empathy is the practice of understanding and empathizing with your own thoughts, feelings, and experiences. Recognize your defects and pardon yourself for botches.

● **Goal Setting:** Put forth attainable objectives that challenge you to develop and foster new abilities. Commend your achievements.

● **Body Inspiration body positivity:** It is a movement that encourages self-acceptance and self-love regardless of one' body shape. Shift your concentration from appearance to well-being and prosperity. Value your body for its solidarity and the astounding things it can do.

● **Personal Boundaries:** Personal boundaries are the limits and guidelines we establish in our interactions with others to protect our physical, emotional, and mental well-being. They define what is acceptable and unacceptable behavior in our relationships and help ensure that we are treated with respect and dignity. Setting and maintaining personal boundaries is essential for healthy relationships and self-care. Learn to establish and maintain personal boundaries, ensuring that you are respected and treated with dignity in all your relationships.

Key aspects of personal boundaries:

1. Know the various types of boundaries:

Physical Boundaries: These define the physical space around you and what is considered appropriate in terms of touch and personal space.

Emotional Boundaries: Emotional boundaries pertain to your feelings and emotional well-being. They involve setting limits on how much you share or how much you allow others to affect your emotions.

Mental Boundaries: These boundaries relate to your thoughts, beliefs, and values. They involve asserting your right to your own opinions and ideas.

Time Boundaries: Time boundaries determine how you allocate your time and energy. They help you prioritize your commitments and avoid overextending yourself.

2. know the 'how' on setting boundaries:

Be clear about your own needs and limits.

Communicate your boundaries with honesty and assertiveness.

Use "I" statements to express your feelings and needs.

For example, *"I need some personal space right now."*

Be consistent in enforcing your boundaries.

3. know how to respect others' boundaries:

- Acknowledge and respect the boundaries of others, just as you expect them to respect yours.

- Ask for permission or consent when entering someone else's personal space or discussing sensitive topics.

4. know the consequences and accountability:

- Clearly communicate the consequences when someone crosses your boundaries.

- Be prepared to enforce consequences if necessary.

- Take responsibility for maintaining your boundaries and standing up for yourself.

5. know when to adjust boundaries:

- It's okay to adjust your boundaries as your needs or circumstances change.

- Regularly evaluate and adapt your boundaries to ensure they are in alignment with your well-being and personal growth.

6. know the boundary violations:

- Recognize signs of boundary violations, such as feeling uncomfortable, disrespected, or overwhelmed.

- Address violations promptly by asserting your boundaries and expressing your feelings.

Remember that healthy boundaries are not about being distant or unkind; they are about creating respectful and mutually beneficial relationships. Boundaries are a sign of self-respect and self-worth, and they contribute to healthier, more fulfilling connections with others.

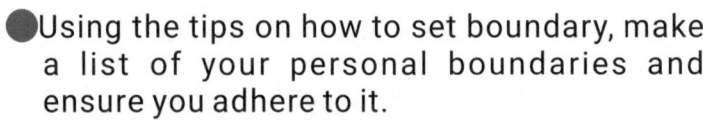

Mindfulness and self-care: Setting and maintaining boundaries is a form of self-care. Practice care to remain present at the time and participate in taking care of oneself exercises that sustain your psychological, close to home, and actual prosperity.

To Do:

Using the tips on how to set boundary, make a list of your personal boundaries and ensure you adhere to it.

NOTE: Every girl is unique, and the step to building self-esteem is personal.

Chapter Two
You Are a Work of Art

Chapter Two

You Are a Work of Art

Understanding Self-Worth and Embracing Your Uniqueness.

Each person, including every teen girl, is an exceptional show-stopper. It's vital for them to grasp that their exceptional characteristic, quirks and imperfections make them special.

Embracing their independence and praising their disparities is a crucial part of self-esteem.

You are an exceptional work of art! However, do you see the value in your uniqueness?

Do you praise your singularity? Do you adore yourself for what your identity is?

Numerous teen girls battle with self-esteem and confidence. They contrast themselves with others and feel lacking or sub-par. They center around their blemishes and deficiencies and disregard their gifts and accomplishments. They let others characterize them and let them know how they ought to be. They feel unreliable and discontent with themselves.

This isn't the means by which you have the right to feel. You have the right to feel certain and glad for yourself. You have the right to regard and esteem yourself. You have the right to embrace your uniqueness and focus your light.

The concept of self-worth

Self-worth is the sensation of huge worth and respect that you have for yourself by and by. It

does not rely upon others' manner of thinking of you, or how you stand out from others, yet on how you see yourself.

It impacts how you feel, think, act, and interface with others.

Self-worth is impacted by numerous factors, similar to your convictions, values, goals, achievements, frustrations, associations, and experiences.

A piece of these components could uphold yourself, while others could cut it down.

Self-worth isn't fixed or static; it can change after a few times and in different conditions.

Along these lines, it is basic to be familiar with your Self-worth and how it affects your life.

Having a high Self-worth infers that you appreciate and laud your uniqueness and assortment. It infers that you don't condemn yourself remorselessly or outlandishly established on absurd or shallow standards of greatness, accomplishment, or predominance.

It infers that you don't permit others to describe you or limit you. It infers that you don't depend upon others for endorsement or support. It suggests that you are independent and free.

Having a high Self-worth can help you in various ways. It can help you with feeling more perfect and more cheerful with yourself and with others, be all the more evident and expressive with your personality, be all the greater and more confident with your perspective, be more open and curious with your advancing, etc.

Having a low Self-worth infers that you don't appreciate or laud your uniqueness and assortment.

It suggests that you judge yourself severely or ridiculously established on outlandish or shallow standards of heavenliness, accomplishment, or predominance.

It suggests that you let others describe you or limit you. It suggests that you depend upon others for endorsement or support. It infers that you are dependent and restricted.

Having a low Self-worth can hurt you in various ways. It can cause you to feel more abnormal and discontent with yourself and with others, be more fake and brutal with your personality, be more pessimistic and skeptical with your perspective, be more closed and awful with your advancing, etc.

Practices to develop a high self-worth for a teen girl:

- **Practicing self-love:** Treat yourself kindly, gently, generously, compassionately, gratefully, joyfully.

- **Practicing self-care:** Take care of your physical, mental, emotional, social, spiritual needs.

- **Practicing self-improvement:** Learn new skills, acquire new knowledge, explore new interests, pursue new goals.

- **Practicing self-expression:** Share your thoughts, feelings, opinions, values, beliefs, dreams.

● **Practicing self-affirmation:** Praise yourself for your efforts, achievements, qualities, strengths.

● **Practicing self-reflection:** Evaluate yourself honestly, constructively, realistically.

● **Practicing self-forgiveness:** Accept yourself unconditionally, learn from your mistakes and move on.

● **Practicing self-empowerment:** Make your own choices, take responsibility for your actions.

● **Practicing self-respect:** Set healthy boundaries, say no when necessary.

● **Practicing self-esteem soaring:** Celebrate the beauty within and beyond appearance.

How to Appreciate the Beauty That Extends Beyond Mere Appearances?

Girl, you need to do the following to appreciate the beauty that extends beyond mere appearance.

✳ Recognize and celebrate your inner beauty, which includes your personality, your character, your values, your passions, your skills, your talents, your creativity, your intelligence, your wisdom, your kindness, your compassion, your courage, your resilience, and your spirit. These are the qualities that make you who you are and that make you beautiful in a deeper and more meaningful way.

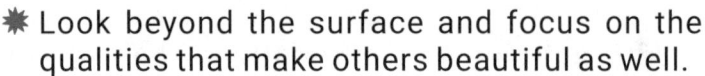

* Look beyond the surface and focus on the qualities that make others beautiful as well.

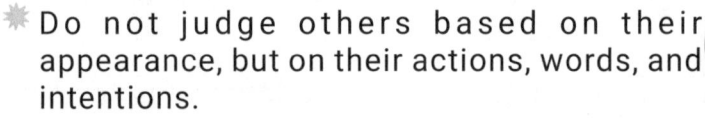

* Do not judge others based on their appearance, but on their actions, words, and intentions.

* Appreciate the diversity and uniqueness of people and cultures. Learn from them and respect them.

* Be kind and supportive to them. Beauty is not a competition or a comparison; it is a collaboration and a celebration.

* Notice and enjoy the beauty of nature, art, music, literature, culture, diversity, humanity, and life itself.

* Be grateful for the beauty that you have and that you can create. Be curious and adventurous about the beauty that you can discover and explore.

* Be creative and expressive about the beauty that you can share and inspire. Beauty is not a limitation or a restriction; it is an opportunity and a possibility.

* Practice self-love and self-care. Treat yourself kindly, gently, generously, compassionately, gratefully, joyfully.

* Take care of your physical, mental, emotional, social, spiritual needs. Do things that make you happy and healthy.

* Do things that challenge you and grow you. Do things that reflect you and respect you.

✹Beauty is not a burden or a pressure; it is a gift and a blessing

To Do:

✹Pause and think of the five things that makes you unique and beautiful.

NOTE: You are beautiful in every way. You are worthy of love and respect. You are unstoppable.

Chapter Three
The Power of Positive Self Talk

Chapter Three

The Power of Positive Self Talk

Mastering the art of self-affirmation, what do you say to yourself when you look in the mirror?

When you face a challenge?

When you make a mistake?

When you achieve a goal?

The words you use to talk to yourself have a powerful impact on your self-esteem. They can either boost your confidence and motivation, or lower your self-worth and happiness.

They can either help you overcome obstacles and pursue your dreams, or hold you back and limit your potential. They can either make you unstoppable, or make you stuck.

Positive self-talk is the practice of using affirming and encouraging words to talk to yourself. It is the act of being your own best friend and cheerleader.

It is the skill of replacing negative and critical thoughts with positive and supportive ones.

Positive self-talk can help you improve your self-esteem in many ways.

Techniques to silence self-doubt and cultivate self-empowering thoughts.

Self-doubt is a common challenge for many teen girls, especially in a society that often pressures them to look and act a certain way.

However, there are some techniques that can help you silence your inner critic and cultivate self-empowering thoughts. Here are some of them:

● Unconditional love. Have permanent love for yourself, regardless of your flaws or mistakes. You are worthy of respect and kindness, no matter what. Remind yourself of this every day, and don't let anyone make you feel otherwise.

● Build up capacity; Develop desirable personal qualities and build your strengths. Learn new skills, pursue your passions, and challenge yourself to grow as a person. Celebrate your achievements and appreciate your efforts.

● Say things to yourself that are kind, positive, or supportive. Replace negative thoughts with more realistic and helpful ones. For example, instead of saying "I can't do this", say "I can do this if I try hard and ask for help when I need it". Use affirmations, such as "I am strong", "I am capable", or "I am beautiful" to boost your confidence.

- Avoid comparisons. Don't compare yourself to others, especially on social media. Everyone has their own strengths and weaknesses, and their own journey in life.

  Focus on your own goals and achievements, and be proud of who you are.

- Surround yourself with people who love you, support you, and inspire you. Talk to your friends, family, teachers, or mentors when you need advice or encouragement. Seek professional help if you struggle with low self-esteem or psychological issues.

To Do:

- Write down ten things that you love about yourself.

- Close your eyes and imagine the most beautiful thing about yourself.

  Take a deep breath in, hold the breath for some seconds ...and breath (repeat this process for two minutes). How did you feel?

NOTE: You are worthy of respect and kindness

Chapter Four
Body Love Revolution

Chapter Four

Body Love Revolution

Embracing body positivity

Your body is amazing. It is the home of your mind, heart, and soul. It is the vehicle of your expression, action, and experience. It is the source of your health, vitality, and pleasure. It is the gift of nature, evolution, and creation.

Your body deserves your love. Not just because it is beautiful, but because it is yours. Not just because it is perfect, but because it is unique. Not just because it is functional, but because it is miraculous.

Body love is when you appreciate, respect, care for, celebrate, and enjoy your body for all that it is and all that it does. Body love helps you to; boost your self-esteem and confidence, reduce your stress and anxiety, enhance your mood and happiness, improve your health and wellness increase your energy and vitality, strengthen your immunity and healing, foster your growth and learning etc.

Body hate is when you criticize, neglect, abuse, shame, or reject your body for all that it is not or all that it does not do. Body hate harms you by; lowering your self-esteem and confidence, increasing your stress and anxiety, diminishing your mood and happiness, impairing your health and wellness, decreasing your energy and vitality, weakening your immunity and healing, hindering your growth and learning etc.

The bad news is that body hate is very common among teen girls.

You may have experienced it yourself or witnessed it among others. You may have been influenced by the unrealistic or superficial standards of beauty that are promoted by the media, the society, or the culture.

You may have been affected by the negative comments or judgments that are made by others or yourself.

The good thing is that you can change how you feel about your body. You can join the body love revolution.

The body love revolution is the movement of people who are reclaiming their right to love their bodies as they are, without conforming to or comparing with any external expectations or norms.

The body love revolution is about:

- Challenging and rejecting the beauty myths and stereotypes that are imposed by the media, the society, or the culture.

- Recognizing and celebrating the beauty and diversity of all bodies, shapes, sizes, colors, abilities, and ages.

- Embracing and expressing your body's uniqueness and personality.

● Nourishing and nurturing your body's needs and desires Protecting and defending your body's rights and boundaries.

Building and boosting self-confidence is a process of developing and enhancing your belief and trust in yourself and your abilities.

It is a process of feeling capable and competent to handle any situation or challenge that you face. It is a process of feeling proud and positive about yourself and your achievements.

Strategies for building a healthy relationship with your body.

Building a healthy relationship with your own body is an important part of being a teen girl.

Your body is changing and growing, and you may have questions or concerns about how you look and feel. You may also face pressure from society, media, or peers to look or act a certain way.

However, you should know that your body is unique and beautiful, and you deserve to love and respect it.

Here are some strategies that can help you build a positive relationship with your own body.

● Appreciate your body for what it can do, not just how it looks. Your body is amazing and capable of many things, such as playing sports, dancing, singing, learning, creating, and more.

Focus on the skills and talents that your body allows you to express, and celebrate your achievements.

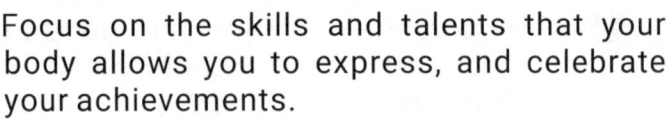

- Avoid comparing yourself to others. Everyone has a different body shape, size, color, and appearance, and that's okay.

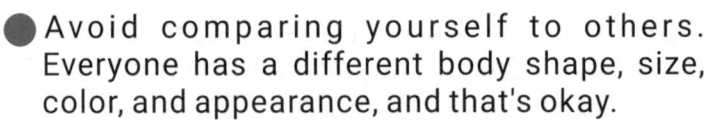

There is no one ideal or perfect way to look or be. Comparing yourself to others can make you feel insecure or unhappy about yourself. Instead, embrace your uniqueness and diversity.

- Challenge negative thoughts and messages.

Sometimes, you may have negative thoughts or feelings about your body, such as "I'm too fat", "I'm too skinny", "I'm ugly", or "I need to change".

These thoughts can be influenced by unrealistic or harmful messages from the media, culture, or peers. However, you should know that these thoughts and messages are not true or helpful.

You can challenge them by replacing them with positive affirmations, such as "I'm beautiful", "I'm strong", "I'm enough", or "I love myself".

- Practice self-care. Taking care of your body is a way of showing respect and love for yourself. You can practice self-care by eating well, staying hydrated, getting enough sleep, exercising regularly, and

relaxing.

You can also pamper yourself with activities that make you feel good, such as taking a bath, getting a massage, listening to music, reading a book-like you are doing now, or doing something creative.

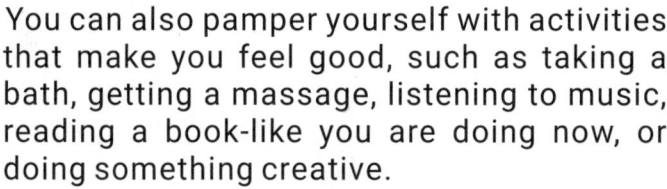

● Seek positive influences. Surround yourself with people who respect you and support you.

They can help you boost your confidence and cope with stress. They can also stand up for you or with you when you face bullying or discrimination.

You can also seek advice from trusted adults, such as parents, teachers, counselors, or mentors (you just got yourself a mentor by reading this book), who can guide you and encourage you… Smile if you want to.

To Do:

● Pen down the number of things that you can do and applaud yourself for that

Chapter Five
Unstoppable Confidence

Unstoppable Confidence

Building and boosting self-confidence.

Confidence is the belief and trust that you have in yourself and your abilities. It is the feeling of being capable and competent to handle any situation or challenge that you face.

It is the feeling of being proud and positive about yourself and your achievements. It is the feeling of being unstoppable!

Confidence can benefit you in many ways, such as; boosting your self-esteem and happiness, enhancing your mood and motivation, improving your performance and productivity, increasing your resilience and coping skills, fostering your growth and learning.

Lack of confidence is the doubt and fear that you have in yourself and your abilities. It is the feeling of being inadequate and incompetent to handle any situation or challenge that you face.

It is the feeling of being ashamed and negative about yourself and your achievements. It is the feeling of being stoppable.

Lack of confidence can harm you in many ways, such as Lowering your self-esteem and happiness. Increasing your stress and anxiety, diminishing your mood and motivation, impairing your performance and productivity, weakening your resilience and coping skills, hindering your growth and learning.

The good news is that you can build and boost your confidence. Confidence is not something that you are born with or without; it is something that you can develop and improve.

Confidence is not something that is fixed or static; it is something that can change and grow.

Confidence is not something that is given or taken; it is something that you can create and maintain you will be able to use confidence as a tool to boost your self-esteem soaring.

You will be able to feel more capable and competent in any situation or challenge. You will be able to feel prouder and more positive about yourself. You will be able to say to yourself: I am confident. I am unstoppable.

Building and boosting self-confidence is a process of developing and enhancing your belief and trust in yourself and your abilities. It is a process of feeling capable and competent to handle any situation or challenge that you face. It is a process of feeling proud and positive about yourself and your achievements.

Some strategies for building and boosting self-confidence are:

- **Identify and analyze your confidence level and sources:** You can use a self-assessment tool, such as the Rosenberg Self-Esteem Scale, to measure your current level of self-confidence and self-esteem.

    You can also identify the sources of your confidence, such as your skills, talents, knowledge, values, goals, etc.

    You can also identify the sources of your lack of confidence, such as your fears, doubts, failures, criticisms, etc.

- **Recognize and overcome obstacles and self-doubt:** Cognitive-behavioral techniques, such as the ABCDE model, can be used to challenge and change your negative thoughts and beliefs that undermine your confidence.

    You can also use coping strategies, such as relaxation, breathing, visualization, etc., to manage your emotions and behaviors that affect your confidence.

- **Positive thinking and affirmations:** You can also use positive thinking to focus on the positive aspects of yourself and your situation, rather than the negative ones.

    Use positive affirmations to reinforce and strengthen your positive beliefs about yourself and your potential. Affirmations are positive statements that reflect your true self and your desired outcomes.

To write effective affirmations for confidence, you can follow these steps:

- Start with "I am" or "I can" to express your identity or ability.

- Use present tense to express your current reality or future intention.

- Use positive words to express your confidence or competence.

- Use specific words to express your goal or action.

- Use realistic words to express your possibility or probability.

- Repeat the affirmation several times with conviction and emotion.

Incorporate confidence into your daily routine:

You can practice confidence by applying it to different areas of your life, such as:

- Practicing new skills or improving existing ones.

- Setting realistic and achievable goals and working towards them.

- Seeking feedback and learning from mistakes.

- Celebrating successes and rewarding yourself.

- Seeking support from positive, supportive, and trustworthy people by using these strategies for building and boosting self-

confidence, you will be able to feel more capable and competent in any situation or challenge.

You will be able to feel more positive about yourself. You will be able to say to yourself: I am confident. I am unstoppable.

To Do:

Write 20 daily affirmations using the steps given in writing "effective affirmations for confidence"

You are to put it on your wall or your door (where it is visible to you).

You can even create a fancy affirmation board for it- do you!

The daily affirmation should become part of your daily routines.

Chapter Six
Navigating the Friendship Maze

Navigating the Friendship Maze

Forming and maintaining healthy friendships.

Navigating the Friendship Maze is one of the most important and rewarding aspects of life. It is the bond of mutual affection, respect, and support that you share with another person.

It is the source of joy, comfort, and growth that you experience with another person. It is the gift of connection, communication, and collaboration that you offer to another person.

Friendship can benefit you in many ways, such as: boosting your self-esteem and happiness, reducing your stress and loneliness, enhancing your mood and motivation, improving your health and wellness, increasing your resilience and coping skills, fostering your growth and learning.

However, friendship can also be challenging and complicated. It is not always easy to find, make, and keep friends. It is not always clear how to deal with conflicts, changes, or differences with friends.

It is not always obvious how to recognize and address toxic relationships with friends.

Toxic relationships are the opposite of healthy friendships. They are the relationships that are harmful, abusive, or manipulative. They are the relationships that drain your energy, lower your confidence, or damage your well-being. They are the relationships that you need to avoid, end, or heal from.

Recognizing and addressing toxic relationships.

Toxic relationships are those that harm your well-being, happiness, or safety.

They can involve physical, emotional, verbal, or sexual abuse, as well as manipulation, control, jealousy, or isolation.

Toxic relationships can affect anyone, but teen girls may be especially vulnerable to them due to peer pressure, low self-esteem, or lack of experience.

Recognizing and addressing toxic relationships is important for teen girls to protect themselves and their mental health. Here are some steps that can help:

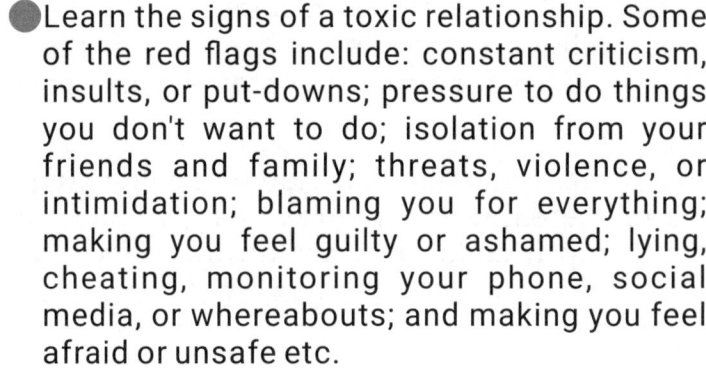

- Learn the signs of a toxic relationship. Some of the red flags include: constant criticism, insults, or put-downs; pressure to do things you don't want to do; isolation from your friends and family; threats, violence, or intimidation; blaming you for everything; making you feel guilty or ashamed; lying, cheating, monitoring your phone, social media, or whereabouts; and making you feel afraid or unsafe etc.

- Trust your instincts and feelings. If something doesn't feel right, don't ignore it or make excuses for it.

  Listen to your gut and pay attention to how you feel around people that are close to you.

  Do you feel happy, respected, and valued? Or do you feel anxious, depressed, and

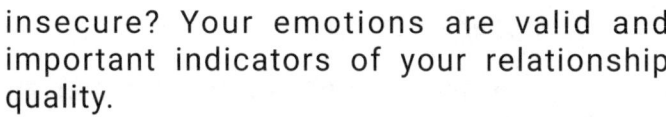

insecure? Your emotions are valid and important indicators of your relationship quality.

- Seek support and help. You are not alone and you don't have to deal with a toxic relationship by yourself.

  Reach out to someone you trust, such as a friend, family member, teacher, counselor, or mentor. They can offer you emotional support, advice, and resources (like this book).

- Set boundaries and end the relationship. You have the right to say no and to end a relationship that is hurting you.

  You don't owe anyone an explanation or a second chance. You deserve to be treated with respect and kindness.

  Setting boundaries means communicating clearly what you want and don't want in a relationship, and sticking to them.

  Ending a relationship means cutting off all contact with that person, blocking them on social media and phone, and avoiding places where they might be.

  It may be hard to do this, but it is necessary for your safety and well-being.

- Heal and move on. Stop being a friend with a toxic person. It can be painful and traumatic. You may experience a range of emotions, such as anger, sadness, guilt, fear, or relief. You may also have flashbacks, nightmares,

or anxiety attacks.

These are normal reactions to an abusive situation and they will get better with time and support.

To heal and move on from a toxic relationship, you need to take care of yourself physically, mentally, and emotionally.

Some of the ways to do this are; getting enough sleep, eating well, exercising regularly, doing things that make you happy, spending time with positive people who love you, seeking therapy or counseling if needed.

To Do:

- Using the red flags of toxic relationship as a checklist, imagine all the people you have around you as friends and family members, is anyone toxic?

  If yes, is it affecting you? If it is, you already know what to do.

- You are to also examine yourself, are you toxic to others?

  If yes, take a step to stop being a toxic friend or a toxic relative or a time will come when you will become lonely.

  no one want to stay around a toxic person for so long.

Chapter Seven
Defying Peer Pressure

Chapter Seven

Defying Peer Pressure

Opposing peer pressure is the capacity to oppose the impact of other people who attempt to cause you to accomplish something that you would rather not do or that is hurtful to you.

Peer strain can be really difficult for anybody, particularly for teenagers and youthful grown-ups who are as yet fostering their personality and values.

In any case, there are a few techniques that can assist you with adapting to peer pressure and make certain, free decisions.

Techniques for resisting negative peer influences/ Making confident, independent choices.

- Know your values and beliefs. Having a clear sense of what is important to you and what you stand for can help you resist peer pressure. You can write down your values and goals and review them regularly to remind yourself of what matters to you.

- Think about the consequences. Before you act on peer pressure, think about the possible outcomes of your actions. Will they benefit you or harm you? Will they affect your health, safety, reputation, or future? Will they violate your morals or laws? If the answer is yes, then you should avoid doing it.

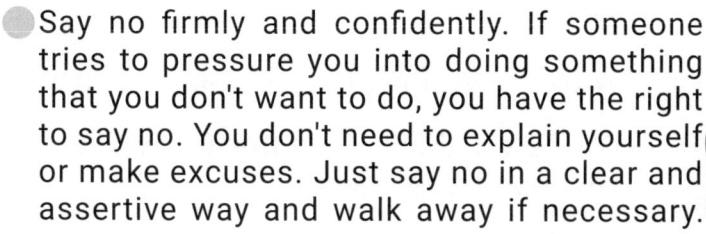

● Say no firmly and confidently. If someone tries to pressure you into doing something that you don't want to do, you have the right to say no. You don't need to explain yourself or make excuses. Just say no in a clear and assertive way and walk away if necessary.

● Seek positive influences. Surround yourself with people who respect your decisions and support your goals. They can help you stay on track and boost your self-esteem. You can also seek advice from trusted adults, such as parents, teachers, counselors, or mentors, who can guide you and encourage you.

● Be a leader, not a follower. Instead of following the crowd, be a role model for others who may be facing peer pressure. You can initiate positive activities that are fun and healthy, such as sports, hobbies, volunteering, or learning new skills. You can also speak up for yourself and others who are being pressured or bullied by peers.

Peer pressure can be a powerful force, but it doesn't have to control your life.

To Do:

Write down your personal values and belief.

Pause and think about the time you ever said **NO** unapologetically.

If you ever did, give yourself a hug and if you have never, ensure you do it, the next time such opportunity comes because you are unstoppable!

NOTE: *Saying NO when it is needed shows you are growing...*

Chapter Eight
Conquering the Bully Battle

Chapter Eight

Conquering the Bully Battle

Addressing bullying in its various forms.

Bullying is a serious problem that can affect many people especially teen girls in different ways. Bullying can be physical, verbal, psychological, or cyberbullying. It can cause harm to the victim's self-esteem, mental health, academic performance, and social relationships. Therefore, it is important to know how to address bullying in its various forms and seek help when needed. Bullying can be addressed in the following ways:

- Tell a trusted adult. If you are being bullied or witness someone else being bullied, you should tell a trusted adult, such as a parent, teacher, counselor, or coach.

  They can help you deal with the situation and protect you from further harm.

- Talk to the bully. Sometimes, the bully may not realize how their actions affect you or others. If you feel safe and comfortable, you can try to talk to the bully privately and calmly.

  Tell them how their words or actions make you feel and ask them to stop. You can also try to understand their perspective and see if there is a way to resolve the conflict peacefully.

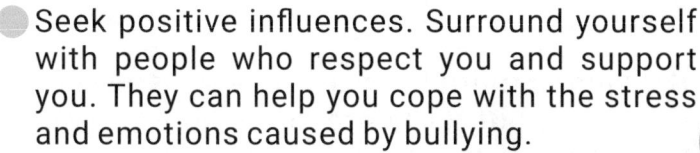 Seek positive influences. Surround yourself with people who respect you and support you. They can help you cope with the stress and emotions caused by bullying.

They can also stand up for you or with you when you face bullying. You can also join clubs, teams, or groups that share your interests and values.

Be assertive. Assertiveness is the ability to express your opinions, feelings, and needs in a respectful and confident way. Assertive people can stand up for themselves and others. Say no to peer pressure, and ask for what you need in a direct manner.

Use a decision-making process. Sometimes making a choice can be overwhelming or confusing when you face bullying. In such cases, for example, you can follow these steps:

1. Identify the problem or situation that requires a decision.

2. Brainstorm possible options or solutions.

3. Evaluate the pros and cons of each option.

4. Choose the best option based on your values and goals.

5. Implement your choice and monitor the results.

6. Learn from your experience and adjust your choice if needed.

Coping strategies for bullying situations.

Bullying situations can be very stressful and upsetting, but there are some coping strategies that can help you deal with them. Here are some of the strategies that can help:

- Seek assistance from an adult, friend, or classmate when a potentially threatening situation occurs.

  Adults in positions of authority, like parents, teachers, or coaches, often can deal with bullying without the bully ever learning how they found out about it.

- Use humor to deflect a potential threatening situation. Humor can be a powerful tool to diffuse tension and show that you are not affected by the bully's words or actions.

  For example, you can make a joke, laugh at yourself, or use sarcasm to respond to a bully.

- Avoid unsafe places or walk away before a potential bullying encounter occurs. Sometimes, the best way to cope with bullying is to avoid it altogether.

  You can try to stay away from places where bullies hang out or where you feel unsafe. You can also walk away or ignore the bully if they try to bother you.

- Talk to the bully. Sometimes, the bully may not realize how their actions affect you or others. If you feel safe and comfortable, you can try to talk to the bully privately and calmly.

Tell them how their words or actions make you feel and ask them to stop. You can also try to understand their perspective and see if there is a way to resolve the conflict.

To Do:

● Do you have a trusted adult that you confide in; that one person that never judges you. If you don' have , you just got yourself one by reading this book: send an email to <u>mtalk2me2@gmail.com</u> introducing yourself by saying I just read your book and I need to talk to you.

NOTE: *Be assertive! staying quiet is not the best way; speak.*

Chapter Nine
Dreams to Reality

Chapter Nine

Dreams to Reality

Goal Setting

Setting and pursuing personal and academic goals is an important skill for a teen girl, as it can help her achieve her dreams and aspirations. Goals are *"specific, measurable, attainable, relevant, and time-bound statements of what you want to accomplish"*.

They can help you focus your efforts, motivate you, and track your progress.
The importance of setting and pursuing personal and academic goals.

- It personalizes the learning process based on your needs. You can choose goals that match your interests, strengths, and challenges.

  You can also adjust your goals as you learn and grow.

- It creates intention and motivation that empowers you. You can set goals that are meaningful and challenging for you.

  You can also celebrate your achievements and learn from your failures.

- It establishes accountability to shift responsibility to you. You can take charge of your own learning and actions. You can also monitor your progress and seek feedback or help when needed.

It provides a foundation for you to advocate for your needs.

You can communicate your goals and expectations to others, such as parents, teachers, or mentors. You can also ask for support or resources that can help you reach your goals.

It improves your self-confidence and self-efficacy. You can develop a positive attitude and belief in your abilities. You can also overcome challenges and obstacles that may come your way

Strategies for turning dreams into achievable objectives.

Visualize your ideal future. Imagine yourself in five or ten years, living the life you want. What are you doing?

Where are you? Who are you with? How do you feel?

Write down your vision in detail and review it often to remind yourself of your purpose

Break down your vision into smaller goals. Think of the steps you need to take to make your vision a reality. What are the short-term, medium-term, and long-term goals that will lead you to your ultimate goal? Write them

down and make sure they are SMART (specific, measurable, attainable, relevant, and time-bound).

- Create an action plan. For each goal, write down the tasks you need to do, the resources you need, the obstacles you may face, and the deadlines you have. Prioritize your tasks and schedule them in your calendar.

- Review your plan regularly and adjust it as needed.

- Monitor your progress and celebrate your achievements. Track your performance and results using tools such as journals, charts, checklists, or apps. Reward yourself for completing your tasks and reaching your milestones. Celebrate your successes and learn from your failures.

- Seek positive influences. Surround yourself with people who respect you and support you. They can help you stay on track and boost your confidence. You can also seek advice from trusted adults, such as parents, teachers, counselors, or mentors, who can guide you and encourage you.

To Do:

✳ Set your personal goals for the week ensuring it is achievable and realistic.

✳ Remember to work towards achieving it. Don' forget to give yourself a hug when you achieve it, and if you did not, you are to carry it over to the next week as you are setting your next weekly goals.

Chapter Ten
Unstoppable You

Chapter Ten

Unstoppable You

Building a Bright Future

The journey ahead and the empowered path forward.

The journey ahead refers to the vision and direction that we have for ourselves and our society. It involves setting goals, making plans, and taking actions that align with our values and aspirations.

It also requires us to be adaptable, resilient, and creative in dealing with the uncertainties and changes that may arise along the way.

Some of the factors that can influence our journey ahead are:

- Our personal and collective well-being. This includes our physical, mental, emotional, and social health, as well as our happiness and satisfaction with life. We need to take care of ourselves and each other, and seek help when we need it.

- Our education and skills. This includes our formal and informal learning, as well as our abilities to think critically, communicate effectively, collaborate with others, and solve problems. We need to keep learning and developing ourselves, and use our skills to contribute to society.

- Our environment and resources. This includes our natural and built surroundings,

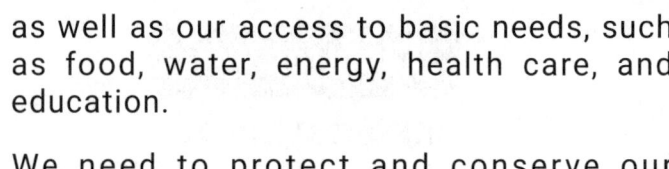

as well as our access to basic needs, such as food, water, energy, health care, and education.

We need to protect and conserve our environment, and use our resources wisely and sustainably.

The empowered path forward refers to the mindset and attitude that we have towards ourselves and our society. It involves believing in ourselves and our potential, as well as supporting others and their potential.

It also requires us to be proactive, responsible, and compassionate in making decisions and taking actions that benefit ourselves and others.

Some of the strategies that can help us build an empowered path forward are;

● **Choosing a growth mindset:** This means having the belief that we can improve ourselves and our situation through our efforts and learning. It also means embracing challenges, learning from feedback, and celebrating progress.

● **Practicing gratitud:** This means being thankful for what we have and what we experience, as well as expressing appreciation to others. It also means focusing on the positive aspects of ourselves and our situation, rather than dwelling on the negative ones.

- **Seeking support and cooperation:** This means reaching out to others who can help us or who share our goals, as well as offering help to others who need it or who can benefit from it.

  It also means working together with others to achieve common objectives.

The vision of an unstoppable, self-assured future.

Building a bright future is a topic that many people are interested in, especially in the face of the challenges and opportunities that our world is facing.

The vision of an unstoppable, self-assured future is one that inspires us to pursue our goals and dreams with confidence and optimism.

According to some sources, there are some steps that can help us create a vision for our future, such as:

- Deepening our self-knowledge by exploring our strengths, values, passions, and purpose.

- Asking ourselves the right questions that can help us clarify our vision, such as "What do I want to achieve in my life?", "What makes me happy and fulfilled?", "What are the obstacles and opportunities that I face?"

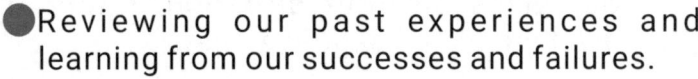Reviewing our past experiences and learning from our successes and failures.

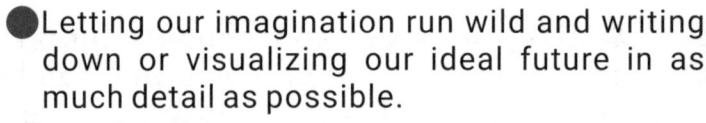Letting our imagination run wild and writing down or visualizing our ideal future in as much detail as possible.

● Planning backwards from our desired future to identify the steps and actions that we need to take to make it happen.

●Choosing new habits that can support our vision and help us overcome any challenges or barriers.

●Creating a vision board or a collage of images, words, or symbols that represent our vision and display it somewhere we can see it often.

●Finding inspiration in the visions of others who have achieved their goals or who share our values and aspirations.

●Summing up our vision in a concise and compelling statement that captures the essence of what we want and why we want it.

NOTE

NOTE

NOTE

NOTE

NOTE

NOTE

NOTE

NOTE

NOTE

NOTE

NOTE

NOTE

NOTE

NOTE

NOTE

NOTE

NOTE

NOTE

Made in United States
Troutdale, OR
11/15/2024

24864169R00046